A Complete Interior Design Company Business Plan:
A Key Part Of How To Start An Interior Design Business

By IN DEMAND BUSINESS PLANS

In Demand Business Plans

Facebook: Facebook/InDemandBusinessPlans

Instagram: @In_Demand_Business_Plans

Twitter: @Twitter In_Demand_BP

Email: InDemandMarketing @ Yahoo.com

Table Of Contents

Introduction

Congratulations on purchasing this book. That may sound odd, but it is a very big step forward to building your business plan and starting your own business. Starting, owning, and operating your own business is not only the American dream, but also the pathway to wealth.

A business plan is critical to establishing the right strategy and to taking the steps needed to ensure your success. Some analysts say a business plan increases the odds of success by four times. Your investment in this business plan is a smart one. As you will see, it will only contribute to your success.

This book, unlike so many others written about business plans, has actually done most of the work for you. While most books are vague and just point you in the right direction, sometimes those directions can get you more lost than you already were. This book is not a basic template. This book takes a completed Interior Design Company Business Plan and provides it to you with all the additional information you will need to complete your own. Rather than a one sentence explanation for each section that directs you to write down all the details about staffing, the needed facility, and long term plans, we have done it for you. We have put together all the details you need and you can use them word for word. Sure you might want to tweak it, but the wording is all there. We don't tell you to write a section on Management. Instead we wrote it for you.

Furthermore, the pictures included show the cover sheet and financial statements needed to complete the plan for a banker or investor. Rather than tell you to include a Revenue Stream Percent to Total Revenue pie chart, we show you what it should look like.

Our management staff of executives and serial entrepreneurs has built the entire plan so you don't have to. The fancy words and terms have all been included for you, which will allow you to focus less on building a plan and more on putting it into action.

First, we recommend that you sit down and read the plan all the way through. As you may see in the table of contents, there are 15 sections to a complete business plan. It should take about thirty minutes to read the entire book. Don't worry. You do not need to understand every word the first time through. But this will help you understand how it all goes together.

As you will see, the vast majority of your business plan has been completed for you. With a few tweaks and adjustments your completed business plan will be ready to present to a bank or investor to secure the start-up funding needed to make your dreams come true.

TABLE OF CONTENTS

1. EXECUTIVE SUMMARY
2. MARKET ANALYSIS
3. MANAGEMENT
4. STAFF
5. COMPETITION
6. COMPETITIVE ADVANTAGE
7. LEGAL ENTITY
8. FACILITY
9. PRODUCTS
10. TARGET CUSTOMER / MARKETING PLAN
11. FINANCIAL PLAN
12. CASH FLOW / PROJECTIONS
13. ASSUMPUTIONS
14. EXIT STRATEGY
15. SUPPORTING DOCUMENTS

CHAPTER 1:
EXECUTIVE SUMMARY

Section 1 of your business plan should be the Executive Summary. The Executive Summary is a recap of the entire business plan. It is the first thing a banker or investor will read to help them understand what the business plan contains.

Modify the paragraphs below for your business.

Springfield Interior Design will be a start-up service business that will generate revenue with residential design services, commercial design services, and with retail sales. The target customer is women in the 30 to 60 years old range. Women 30 to 50 years old are responsible for 80% of total home and office design planning and related purchases.

Springfield Interior Design will be located in Springfield, Missouri, a city with a population of 160,000, located in the southwest part of the state. While the initial goal is to open one office / retail location, long term plans are to maintain a long term return of investment and/or sell the operation for four times annual earnings.

With a focus on customer service, Springfield Interior Design will have a huge competitive advantage in the regional community and in the industry as a whole. Additional competitive advantage will come from providing a top notch product at a competitive price. Expenses will be controlled and logistics will be established and managed by the owner / operator, who has a long history in the interior design industry.

Springfield Interior Design has an established financial plan to be in the black after the third month of operation and achieve a consistently growing net cash flow by the end of year one. Opportunities will be available to build a solid customer following to support future growth. Springfield Interior Design will be a financially sound, revenue producing business that will be sellable and attractive to buyers who are seeking a solid return on their investment.

CHAPTER 2:
MARKET ANALYSIS

Section 2 should be the Market Analysis. The Market Analysis describes the industry the business will be a part of. It includes a breakdown of the industry into segments and describes the past trends and what is expected in the future.

Modify the paragraphs below for your business.

The interior design industry has annual sales of approximately $13 billion. Top line sales increased by 3% between 2011 and 2016. While many industries have struggled significantly since 2008 with very poor economic conditions, the interior design industry has managed to maintain modest incremental sales. Considering that the overall economic environment is slowly improving, the interior design industry is in a great position going forward. Some analysts predict that the home lighting industry could see continued sales growth through 2022.

Competition in the interior design industry is extremely segmented. The industry is made up almost exclusively of independent operations, many times with two or fewer employees. The five largest firms in the U.S. make up less than 10% of total industry revenue.

The industry is unique in its large number of operations, while remaining segmented and independent. It has historically been, and remains, primarily a mom and pop operation industry. This holds true both for the lack of national or regional chains and for the amount of one person operations. Currently, there are approximately 103,000 interior design businesses (documented) with less than 128,000 employees. That is an average of less than 1.24 employees per business, including the owner / operator. Statistics show that over 82% of interior design businesses operate with less than 5 employees and nearly 70% operate with less than 3 employees.

CHAPTER 3: MANAGEMENT

Section 3 of your business plan should be Management. This section gives a brief history of the owner or owners, their related work experience, and the skills they possess to own and operate their own business.

Modify the paragraphs below for your business.

Mary Smith received her Bachelor of Science degree in Business Studies, with a minor in Interior Design, from Drury University in Springfield, Missouri. She has ten years of experience in the interior design and home décor retail industry, working five years in retail sales and spending the last five years in interior design management.

As a lifelong home décor and designer enthusiast, Mrs. Smith has extensive knowledge of home furnishings, home décor, interior design, and the brands that are prevalent in the industry. She also has extensive knowledge of trends, as well as staple items that always sell well year after year. Furthermore, Mrs. Smith volunteers in her spare time at community centers and senior centers, working to promote attractive home and community designs on a budget.

As owner and operator of Springfield Interior Design, Mrs. Smith will be directly involved in all the day to day operations. This hands on approach will allow her to fully understand the wants and needs of the target customer and in turn, stock and merchandise the retail space accordingly. It will be vital to remain in touch with the industry, the national selling trends, as well as the local interest.

Mrs. Smith will also oversee all management and financial processes of the operation. This includes, but is not limited to, the design plans, the inventory purchasing, merchandising, the monthly budget and expenses, the P&L, staff training, and any future expansion. Her previous job training and educational background provide the needed framework to excel in these areas.

CHAPTER 4:
STAFF

Section 4 should be Staff. The Staff section will outline the number of employees, their job duties, the required training, as well as the specific responsibilities of the owner.

Modify the paragraphs below for your business.

Mrs. Smith will be the owner / operator of Springfield Interior Design at its inception. This will allow her to be present and fine-tune the logistics of daily operations. Mrs. Smith will also be able to lay the framework needed for future growth and expansion.

In part due to the hours of operation outlined in the following sections Mrs. Smith will not be able to operate Springfield Interior Design on an ongoing basis alone. She will employ one full-time employee to assist with design, sales, customer service, and store maintenance.

At the end of year one, Springfield Interior Design will be operated with two full-time employees, with Mrs. Smith providing all staff training and managerial guidance. Mrs. Smith will still oversee all management and financial processes. This includes, but is not limited to, the monthly budget and expenses, the P&L, and the expansion to additional locations.

At the end of year two, Springfield Interior Design will be operated with three full-time employees. The role of Mrs. Smith will be the same. The additional employee will assist with the increase in design needs and retail sales.

All employees will need to be trained to assist customers, operate the register, handle money, and maintain the standards of the business. This knowledge will be critical for all employees. Great customer service, provided in part with extensive knowledge of the product and services, will help Springfield Interior Design build customer loyalty and encourage repeat business.

CHAPTER 5:
COMPETITION

Section 5 of your business plan should be Competition. This section outlines the competition in the local community. It describes the top two to four competitors and explains their strengths and weaknesses.

Modify the paragraphs below for your business.

Competition in the interior design industry is extremely segmented. The industry is made up almost exclusively of independent operations, many times with two or fewer employees. The five largest firms in the U.S. make up less than 10% of total industry revenue.

The industry is unique in its large number of operations, while remaining segmented and independent. It has historically been, and remains, primarily a mom and pop operation industry. This holds true both for the lack of national or regional chains and for the amount of one person operations. Currently, there are approximately 103,000 interior design businesses (documented) with less than 128,000 employees. That is an average of less than 1.24 employees per business, including the owner / operator. Statistics show that over 82% of interior design businesses operate with less than 5 employees and nearly 70% operate with less than 3 employees.

Even with relatively low barriers to entry, interior design businesses are an uncommon first time business for many entrepreneurs. They are rarely started by anyone who is not formally educated in interior design and prefers freelance work over working for an established company. This, of course, leads to the segmentation of the market.

A+ Designs is the perfect example of a traditional interior design business in the Springfield metro area. An owner / operator operation, it offers adequate work and average prices. And like most of the independent businesses in the industry, A+ Designs lacks when it comes to customer service. While the owner / operator is a nice person, she is responsible for taking calls, scheduling appointments, offering quotes, doing the work, sending invoices, and providing follow up, in addition to planning the marketing, maintaining the website, maintaining the equipment and vehicle, and everything else that is required to manage a business. Customer service, unfortunately, is the easiest task to disregard the importance of, so it, therefore, is often not given the attention it needs.

Interior Designs 4 U is a similar business in the Springfield metro area. While A+ Designs offers adequate work at an average price, Interior Designs U offers slightly less adequate work at similar points. Interior Designs 4 U focuses on the customer service aspect that A+ Designs misses, but fails to offer a superior or even equivalent product. Where A+ Designs falters on customer service, Interior Designs 4 U fails to provide excellent work or completed work in a timely manner. While the owner and staff is personable, energetic, and a pleasure to work with, their delivery of quotes, ideas, or executed designs often leaves room for improvement.

Locations & Hours of Operation

INTERIOR DESINGS 4 U

3620 S. National, Springfield, MO. 65807

417-866-2453

Mon-Fri: 10:00 – 6:00

Sat-Sun: By Appointment Only

A+ DESIGNS

1926 E. Sunshine, Springfield, MO. 65804

417-883-1113

Mon-Fri: 10:00 – 6:00

Sat-Sun: By Appointment Only

CHAPTER 6:
COMPETITIVE ADVANTAGE

Section 6 should be Competitive Advantage. The Competitive Advantage of your business is the one thing, or two, or possible more, that will set you apart from your competition and make you successful. This is an important section for seeking funding from a bank or investor.

Modify the paragraphs below for your business.

Springfield Interior Design will have three distinct advantages over the competition. Together they will ensure its success well into the future.

The first critical advantage for Springfield Interior Design will be the quality of work. Mrs. Smith has an extensive education and job experience, to create an incredible foundation going forward. By providing creative, inspiring, and extremely well put together projects, in a timely manner, Springfield Interior Design will attract customers and be the dominant competitor in the Springfield metro area.

The second critical advantage for Springfield Interior Design will be the level of customer service provided. Creative, inspiring, and extremely well put together projects will be less well received and will do little to build the business without exception customer service. While the completion may focus on the work, Springfield Interior Design will focus on the customer, ensuring they receive top quality work and top quality service. The customer must feel welcome, understood, and must feel like their vision is being executed. Great work will only be viewed as great if the customer feels properly serviced.

The third competitive advantage is price. While the interior design sector has a vast price range for services, there is certainly competition for price nonetheless. Springfield Interior Design will provide high quality products, with high quality service, at very competitive pricing. The elitist competition consistently overvalues your products and services and therefore overcharges for routine projects. While there is ample opportunity to drive margin on key projects, standard services provided should be viewed as customer and volume builders and be priced as such.

CHAPTER 7:
LEGAL ENTITY

Section 7 of your business plan should be Legal Entity. This section describes how your business will be legally organized within your state. It also includes a list of local licenses that may be required and their approximate cost.

Modify the paragraphs below for your business.

Springfield Interior Design could be organized as an S Corporation or LLC. Either would provide the structure needed for operations. While there are differences, the key characteristic of each are the same.

Both an S Corporation and LLC offer limited liability to the owners. This limited liability means the owners will not be personally responsible for the debts and liabilities of the business.

While the filing process may be different for each they remain the same in offering pass-through taxation. This means that even if Springfield Interior Design is required to file a tax return no taxes will actually be paid at the corporation level. With either an S Corporation or LLC Mrs. Smith will move the business profit to her personal taxes.

This avoids being taxed twice; at the business level and the personal level.

Both are also similar in their quarterly and annual requirement by the state. These are limited to submitting basic information so the state knows you are still in operation.

Regardless of the structure, Springfield Interior Design will file for and receive a Federal Identification Number as well as a State Sales Tax License.

Additional legal requirements will include the following licenses and their estimated costs.

City License

$24.00 per year

County License

CHAPTER 8:
FACILITY

Section 8 should be Facility. The Facility is a description of the actual building or store needed to make your business successful. It includes the needed square footage, the most desired intersections, and anything specific that needs to be considered for this business.

Modify the paragraphs below for your business.

Springfield Interior Design will be a brick and mortar operation in Springfield, Missouri. Springfield is a city with a population of 160,000 in the southwest part of the state. It is the center of a metro area with a population of 400,000.

Springfield Interior Design will be open seven days a week from 10:00 a.m. – 8:00 p.m..

The flagship store will be a free standing location or in a strip shopping center. Either one will require the same basic needs to make Springfield Interior Design a success.

* Springfield Interior Design must be 4,000 square feet.

*At least 1,000 square feet must be dedicated to presentation space.

At least 2,000 square feet must be dedicated to the showroom.

Approximately 600 square feet must be dedicated to freight processing and back stock.

The location must be a glass front building or unit for better visibility by customers.

The location must be on a high traffic road, near a high traffic intersection, in a commercial district. An ideal location would be near S. Glenstone & Sunshine or S. Campbell & Republic Rd.

The rent is estimated to be 4,000 per month, or approximately $1.00 per square foot.

CHAPTER 9:
PRODUCTS

Section 9 of your business plan should be Products. Products describe the actual products you will sell or the services you provide to generate revenue. It includes a breakdown of what percentage of total revenue that each revenue source will be.

Modify the paragraphs below for your business.

Service

As the name suggests, Springfield Interior Design will be an interior design service company. These services will include new build projects to remodels, both for commercial and non-commercial customers.

Springfield Interior Design will have revenue streams from three primary categories. The first two, Residential Design Services and Commercial Design Services make up 80% of total income. This will be done by offering staple design services, as well as more extensive project services, at competitive prices.

Residential Design services will edge Commercial slightly with 45% of total revenue. This is due to the focus on these staple services, and by driving the price points that will reach a wider range of the population and customer base.

Top selling services offered are as follows:

*Room Remodels

*Décor Selection

*Art Selection

*Color Platforms

*Seating Conformity

*Space Saving Plans

*Concierge Shopping Service

*Basic Design Plan Layouts

*Extensive Design Plan Layouts – including spec pics

*Complete Project Managers

*Dorm Room Design

*And much more.

Products

The third revenue producer for Springfield Interior Design is Merchandise Sales at 20%. This revenue stream will be driven by the hand selected, core products featured in the Springfield Interior Design showroom. With staged scenes from a bedroom, bathroom, kitchen, lounging space, and office, Springfield Interior Design will prominently display select products that will be available for purchase.

Top selling product lines that must be considered are as follows:

*Staple Bedding

*Staple Window Treatments

*Lighting

*Small Furniture: including entryway tables and decorative accessories

*Seasonal Décor

*Frames

*Art Prints

*Decorative Pillows

*Throw Pillows

*Staple Washroom Linens

*Bath Ensembles

*Contemporary Desk Accessories

*Space Savers / Storage

*Accent Rugs

*And many more

CHAPTER 10:
TARGET CUSTOMER/ MARKETING

Section 10 should be the Target Customer / Marketing. This section describes specifically who your target customer is, based upon industry analysis and your competitive advantage. It also includes a detailed breakdown of each avenue you will use to attract customers.

Modify the paragraphs below for your business.

Target Customer

The target customer is women in the 30 to 60 years old range. Women 30 to 50 years old are responsible for 80% of total home and office design planning and related purchases.

Marketing Plan

The initial grand opening will be marketed using radio spots on key stations for two weeks. This will be sufficient in notifying the public that Springfield Interior Design has opened and provide the location address.

After the initial opening, Springfield Interior Design will expand and utilize the following seven areas for marketing and growth.

1. The Sign on the building. This will be critical due to the stores high traffic location. The signs will be visible to thousands of people a day and can provide great name recognition and some spontaneous foot traffic.

2. Signs in the Windows. Signs in the windows will advertise specific types of services.

3. Direct Mailing. Sending a postcard mailer directly to people's homes will be a great way to establish name recognition and customer interest. In a simple, easy to follow mailer, Springfield Interior Design will clearly list the name, the address, key categories, and the appealing price points. The mailing will be processed through a local mailing company that specializes in retail mailings and will be narrowed down to the sector of the community that most fits the target customer.

4. Brochures and business cards. There will be two stacks on the counter to assist each customer during and after their visit. The first will be Springfield Interior Design business cards. They will assist the customer in remembering the name and location. The second will be pricing guides. These outline the categories of products and accessories that Springfield Interior Design sells in its store and the price they sell for. These will be updated regularly to showcase new arrivals, hot sellers, and seasonal merchandise.

5. Repeat customers will be an essential part of continued growth. With a pricing structure and store décor that is inviting, customers will return annually, after their initial visit.

6. The Springfield Interior Design website (www.SpringfieldDesign.com) will show the exterior and interior of the business, displaying the massive variety of inventory in real world setting and the comfortable environment. The website will present services provided and how the store is utilized. Images of the showroom, along with descriptions of the store and its massive assortment will clearly represent Springfield Interior Design as a top notch interior design company, for both residential and commercial customers. The site will press heavily on the pricing structure, primarily displaying the low opening price point of staple services and items, as well as promoting the upcoming seasons.

7. In the last decade Social Media has become a critical part of most Marketing Plans including this one. A Facebook page will be established and utilized to promote price points, show new arrivals, and provide other basic information to drive customers into the store. An average of four posts a day will keep the information flowing appropriately. YouTube, Twitter, LinkedIn, Snapchat, and others will also be considered for use as well. This will be critical to attract all customers, but particularly the 30 to 40 year old age group. Posts must be clever, catchy, but emphasis the value of Springfield Interior Design.

CHAPTER 11:
FINANCIAL PLAN

Section 11 of your business plan should be the Financial Plan. The first page of the Financial Plan describes the funding that will be needed to start the business and explains how the money will be spent. The second page is a spreadsheet detailing each start-up cost and a bar graph to display each items percentage to total expenses.

Modify the paragraphs below for your business.

Springfield Interior Design will seek outside financing for this new venture. Startup costs are estimated to be approximately $100,000 and will be funded in part by the owner / operator (20%) and in part through a bank loan or private investor funding (80%).

The inventory needed will make up 31% of the total start-up cost. It will be the most significant start-up expense. This is to ensure that the showroom is complete with the correct products, brands, and overall assortments. The fixtures, at 12%, are the second most significant expense. These fixtures will allow all products to be properly displayed in a natural, home or office design, and will provide the most positive viewing experience possible for customers. The marketing plan and the initial vehicle lease payment are the third and fourth largest expenses, each at 10%. As outlined in the previous section, multiple marketing avenues will be utilized to maximize public awareness and drive customers to the office.

It is projected that Springfield Interior Design will reach the breakeven point at the end of the third month of operations. It will then remain in the black, month after month, indefinitely. With the correct purchasing policy, Springfield Interior Design will maintain a profit margin of 50%.

Because Mrs. Smith is included as a paid employee, the owners return on investment is, at least in part, included in the projected labor expenses. Therefore, all projected net profits can be reinvested in the business for expansion and to grow of the brand.

Springfield Interior Design does not see a required increase in fixed cost due to an increase in sales volume. Expenses like rent, utilities, telephone, and so on, will remain the same at start-up, six months, and well beyond the first year in business. Expenses like labor and marketing may increase, but are controlled expenses. And any additional inventory expenses will be directly tied to additional sales.

The second page of Section 11: Financial Plan should be a spreadsheet outlining the specific start-up costs and their percentage of the total start-up cost. A pie chart is always ideal for displaying these expenses. The following picture shows these for Springfield Interior Design.

PROJECTED STARTUP COST

PROJECTED STARTUP COST			
INITIAL LEASE PAYMENTS AND DEPOSITS	$	8,000.00	8%
LEASEHOLD IMPROVEMENTS	$	1,000.00	1%
SECURITY DEPOSITS	$	1,200.00	1%
FIXTURES	$	12,000.00	12%
INVENTORY	$	31,400.00	31%
INITIAL VEHICLE LEASE PAYMENT / DEPOSIT	$	10,000.00	10%
VEHICLE LOGO / WRAP	$	1,000.00	1%
OPENING SUPPLIES	$	800.00	1%
INSURANCE	$	400.00	0%
LICENSE / PERMITS	$	200.00	0%
MARKETING BUDGET	$	10,000.00	10%
MISCELLANEOUS AND UNFORSEEN COSTS	$	4,000.00	4%
WORKING CAPITAL	$	20,000.00	20%
TOTAL STARTUP COSTS	**$**	**100,000.00**	**100%**

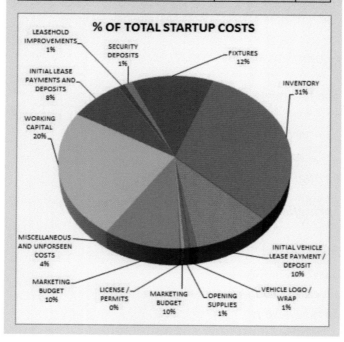

% OF TOTAL STARTUP COSTS

CHAPTER 12:
CASH FLOW/ PROJECTIONS

Section 12 should be the Cash Flow / Projections. This is the largest section of the plan, with a total of nine pages that cover all the financial details about the business. The first page of the section will explain and recap the spreadsheets and graphs that follow. The spreadsheets and graphs include a revenue analysis, breakeven point, a one year monthly P&L, one, two, and three year P&L's, a balance sheet, and one, three, and five year income graphs.

Modify the paragraphs below for your business.

The following pages include multiple tables and graphs to outline the financial projections and potential cash flow of Springfield Interior Design. Each one utilizes the plans and projections included throughout each section of the business plan.

Springfield Interior Design will have revenue streams from three primary retail categories. The first and most prominent is Residential Design Services at 45% of total income. The second largest revenue producer is Commercial Design Services at 35%. These two groups will be driven by professional design services and exceptional customer service.

The third revenue producer is Retail Sales at 20%. While the assortment will be focused upon width, rather than depth, the products types offered will be core staple goods, top performing brands, personality based product lines, and great values, as well as trendy, new goods. These items will utilized in design presentations to both drive retail sales and maximize the all-inclusive service provided.

The Proforma First Year Monthly Profit & Loss outlines the first twelve months of operations. The projected gross income at the top of each month will produce the projected net profit at the bottom. As previously stated, Springfield Interior Design will meet the financial breakeven point at the end of the third month. To do this a monthly gross income of less than $30,000 is required.

On the Proforma Profit & Loss table three years of gross income, expenses, and net profit are presented. It is important to note that expenses like the lease and utilities remain unchanged or virtually unchanged even with a significant increase in gross income. Other expenses, like labor and marketing, increase significantly over the three years, but remain in proportion to the gross income and net profit.

The Proforma Balance Sheet show the slight increase in inventory requirements over three years, but highlights the significant growth in owners' equity for the same period of time.

The final three line graphs show monthly or quarterly gross income for one, three, and five years. The breakeven point is also marked on each to show its relation to gross income.

The pictures below show these financial statements and graphs for Springfield Interior Design.

% OF TOTAL REVENUE

% OF TOTAL REVENUE	
RESIDENTIAL DESIGN SERVICES	45%
COMMERCIAL DESIGN SERVICES	35%
RETAIL SALES	20%
	100%

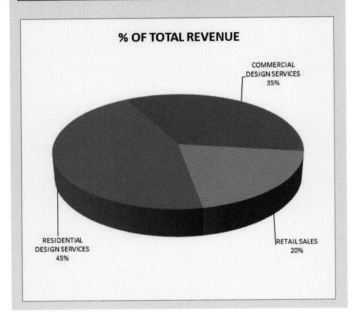

34

MONTHLY PROFIT OR (LOSS)
BREAKEVEN POINT

OPERATING INCOME		
GROSS REVENUE	$	27,176.00
COGS	$	13,588.00
NET REVENUE	$	13,588.00
OPERATING COST		
LABOR	$	4,773.00
LOAN PAYMENT	$	1,585.00
LEASE	$	4,000.00
UTILITIES	$	400.00
VEHICLE LEASE	$	500.00
FUEL	$	200.00
TELEPHONE/ DSL	$	85.00
INSURANCE	$	33.00
BOOKKEEPING	$	75.00
ADVERTISING	$	1,434.00
CREDIT CARD FEES	$	451.00
LICENSE / PERMITS	$	17.00
TRASH REMOVAL	$	20.00
MAINTENANCE & REPAIRS	$	15.00
SUPPLIES	$	50.00
WEBSITE	$	10.00
TOTAL EXPENSES	$	13,588.00
NET PROFIT OR LOSS	$	-

PROFORMA FIRST YEAR MONTHLY PROFIT AND LOSS

MONTH	1	2	3	4	5	6	7	8	9	10	11	12	TOTAL
GROSS REVENUE	24,000	25,000	27,200	28,000	29,000	30,000	32,000	34,000	36,000	38,000	40,000	43,000	386,200
COGS	12,000	12,500	13,600	14,000	14,500	15,000	16,000	17,000	18,000	19,000	20,000	21,500	193,100
NET REVENUE	12,000	12,500	13,600	14,000	14,500	15,000	16,000	17,000	18,000	19,000	20,000	21,500	193,100
OPERATING COST													
LABOR	4,773	4,773	4,773	4,773	4,773	4,773	4,773	4,773	4,773	4,773	4,773	4,773	57,276
LOAN PAYMENT	1,585	1,585	1,585	1,585	1,585	1,585	1,585	1,585	1,585	1,585	1,585	1,585	19,020
LEASE	4,000	4,000	4,000	4,000	4,000	4,000	4,000	4,000	4,000	4,000	4,000	4,000	48,000
UTILITIES	400	400	400	400	400	400	400	400	400	400	400	400	4,800
VEHICLE LEASE	500	500	500	500	500	500	500	500	500	500	500	500	6,000
FUEL	200	200	200	200	200	200	200	200	200	200	200	200	2,400
TELEPHONE / DSL	85	85	85	85	85	85	85	85	85	85	85	85	1,020
INSURANCE	33	33	33	33	33	33	33	33	33	33	33	33	396
BOOKKEEPING SERVICES	75	75	75	75	75	75	75	75	75	75	75	75	900
ADVERTISING	1,434	1,434	1,434	1,434	1,434	1,434	1,434	1,434	1,434	1,434	1,434	1,434	17,208
CREDIT CARD FEES	250	300	340	390	430	470	490	500	535	555	570	582	5,412
LICENSE / PERMITS	204	0	0	0	0	0	0	0	0	0	0	0	204
TRASH REMOVAL	20	20	20	20	20	20	20	20	20	20	20	20	240
MAINTENANCE & REPAIR	15	15	15	15	15	15	15	15	15	15	15	15	180
SUPPLIES	50	50	50	50	50	50	50	50	50	50	50	50	600
WEBSITE	10	10	10	10	10	10	10	10	10	10	10	10	120
TOTAL EXPENSES	13,634	13,420	13,460	13,510	13,550	13,590	13,610	13,620	13,655	13,675	13,690	13,702	163,776
NET PROFIT OR (LOSS)	-1,634	-920	140	490	950	1,410	2,390	3,380	4,345	5,525	6,310	7,798	29,324

36

PROFORMA PROFIT AND LOSS (YEARLY)

YEAR	1	2	3
GROSS REVENUE	384,000	541,200	700,000
COGS	192,000	270,600	350,000
NET REVENUE	192,000	270,600	350,000

OPERATING COST

	1	2	3
LABOR	57,280	85,920	114,560
LOAN PAYMENT	19,020	19,020	19,020
LEASE	48,000	48,000	48,000
UTILITIES	4,800	5,040	5,292
VEHICLE LEASE	6,000	6,000	6,000
FUEL	2,400	2,400	2,400
TELEPHONE / DSL	1,020	1,080	1,140
INSURANCE	396	444	444
BOOKKEEPING SERVICE	900	960	1,020
ADVERTISING	17,204	24,660	32,140
CREDIT CARD FEES	5,412	6,504	7,800
LICENSE / PERMITS	204	300	396
TRASH REMOVAL	240	240	240
MAINTENANCE & REPAIRS	180	276	408
SUPPLIES	600	804	996
WEBSITE	120	120	120
TOTAL EXPENSES	163,776	201,768	239,976

NET PROFIT OR (LOSS)	28,224	68,832	110,024

PROFORMA BALANCE SHEET (YEARLY)

YEAR	1	2	3
ASSETS			
CASH	28,224	68,832	110,024
ACCOUNTS RECEIVABLE	0	0	0
FIXTURES	12,000	12,000	12,000
INVENTORY	42,800	45,000	50,000
LEASE DEPOSITS	4,000	4,000	4,000
SECURITY DEPOSITS	1,200	1,200	1,200
WEBSITE	200	200	200
TOTAL ASSETS	**88,424**	**131,232**	**177,424**
LIABILITIES			
BUSINESS LOAN	66,153	51,304	35,380
ACCOUNTS PAYABLE	0	0	0
LONG TERM LIABILITIES	0	0	0
OTHER LIABILITIES	0	0	0
TOTAL LIABILITIES	**66,153**	**51,304**	**35,380**
EQUITY			
OWNERS EQUITY	22,271	79,928	142,044
TOTAL EQUITY	**22,271**	**79,928**	**142,044**
TOTAL LIABILITIES & EQUITY	**88,424**	**131,232**	**177,424**

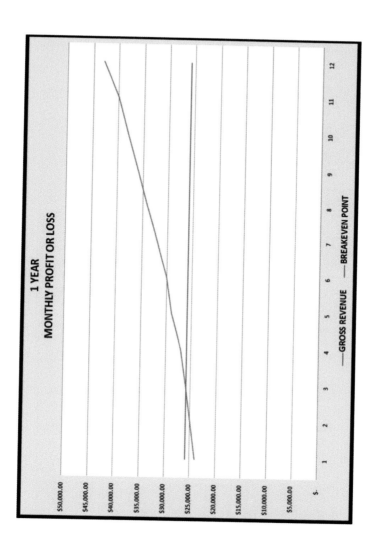

1 YEAR
MONTHLY PROFIT OR LOSS

GROSS REVENUE   BREAKEVEN POINT

39

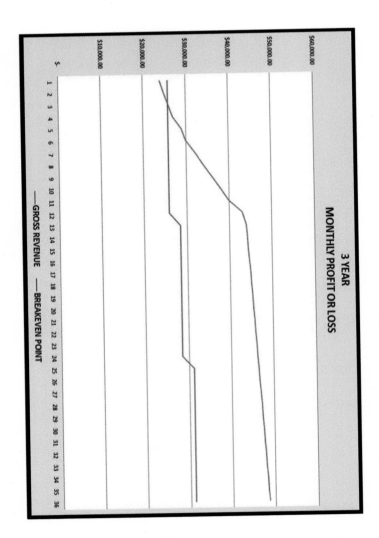

3 YEAR
MONTHLY PROFIT OR LOSS

GROSS REVENUE ——— BREAKEVEN POINT

40

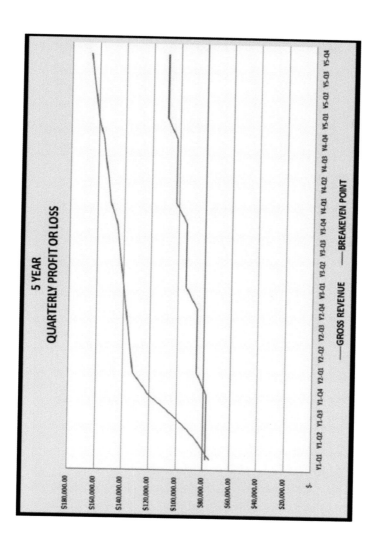

5 YEAR
QUARTERLY PROFIT OR LOSS

GROSS REVENUE ——— BREAKEVEN POINT

CHAPTER 13:
ASSUMPTIONS

Section 13 should be Assumptions. The Assumptions are a list of things one must assume when planning to start their own business. It is simple section, but should be included.

Modify the paragraphs below for your business.

The projections and business strategy provided in this business plan are based upon assumptions that the economy, consumer spending habits, and population growth in the Springfield metro area will continue for the foreseeable future.

Springfield Interior Design must also assume that its present and future suppliers will continue to sell inventory at prices that allow for maintaining present or similar margins.

It is also important that the job market allows Springfield Interior Design to hire reliable employees at reasonable wages. This should not be a concern because the availability of mid-range design employees as well as the mid-range retail employees has always remained vast.

Springfield Interior Design must also assume that the interior design, home furnishings, and home décor industry will remain constant, allowing the free enterprise market to sustain itself. It is assumed that no policy or legislation at the state or federal level will be implemented that would disrupt, prohibit, or heavily burden the sale or ownership of interior design, home furnishings, or home décor, products, related items, or services.

CHAPTER 14:
EXIT STRATEGY

Section 14 should be the Exit Strategy. This business plan is written as a long term investment that could be sold in the future.

Modify the paragraphs below for your business.

Springfield Interior Design will grow to be the number one interior design company in southwest Missouri for its intended target market. All decisions and strategic planning are designed to build the business as a long term investment. Springfield Interior Design will be developed and managed to provide the owners with a consistent and significant return on their investment month after month and year after year.

Furthermore, as the business grows and continues to provide a consistent increase in the annual net profit, the owner may wish to be less hands-on with daily operations and assume more of an investor's type role. With the proper Standard Operating Procedure in place and the correct store manager, Springfield Interior Design can produce a sizable income with minimal requirements.

A secondary plan is to possibly list Springfield Interior Design for sale with a business broker. This would not take place before the end of one year of operations and the establishment of a consistent net profit. Springfield Interior Design would be valued and listed for four times annual earnings. This business plan, along with the proper Standard Operating Procedure, will allow another investor to purchase Springfield Interior Design and further its success.

CHAPTER 15:
SUPPORTING DOCUMENTS

Section 15 should be the final section of your business plan and should be Supporting Documents. This section should include any additional documents or papers that will support you and your business plan. This includes surveys and studies about the industry or your community and any additional financial documentation needed for seeking funding.

We have included a list of general business definitions as well as an SBA Information Sheet. Visit www.SBA.gov and consult with your local lending officer for documents specific to your needs.

Including information pages, like the Definitions of Terms and SBA Information Sheet, adds validity and girth to your plan. They should always be put at the end of all the other information, as we did by placing them in Section 15: Supporting Documents.

While it isn't critical to read each one now, browse through them quickly, there is more important details that follow.

DEFINITIONS OF TERMS

80 / 20 Rule: The 80 / 20 Rule refers to 80% of the results coming from 20% of the action taken. For example, 80% of retail sales come from 20% of the products. Although it may not always be exactly 80 & 20, it is a great rule of thumb for many business situations.

Accounting Period: An Accounting Period is a period of time, usually a month, quarter, or year, for which a financial statement is prepared.

Accounts Payable: Accounts Payable is accounts representing amounts owed by a business and to whom they are owed. The most common accounts are for debt owed to creditors or suppliers.

Accounts Receivable: Opposite of Account Payable, Accounts Receivable document amounts owed to you from customers or suppliers.

Actuals: Real costs, sales, or other measurable metrics, as opposed to plans, goals, estimates, or expectations.

Anchor Tenant: The primary or most prestigious tenant in an office building or shopping center. These tenants are most commonly identified by occupying the largest percentage of square footage.

Articles Of Association: A document which contains the purpose and general structure of a company, including the duties and responsibilities of key people and roles.

Aspirational Brand: A product (or brand) that is commonly admired or perceived as high quality by consumers or competitors.

Asset: Any property or resources of a person, association, or corporation that pertains value and could be used to pay debts or as leverage in financing is an Asset. This includes, but is not limited to, cash, notes, accounts receivable, inventories, fixtures, machinery, real estate, and possibly trademarks and patents.

Auditor: A qualified or certified person who is tasked with reviewing the financial records of a company for accuracy.

B2B: See Business To Business

B2C: See Business To Consumer

Bait-and-Switch: The inappropriate and potentially illegal act of utilizing advertisement to lure customers under the guise of a particular saving or offering, that is not in fact available, in order to sell them on a higher priced or less valued product.

Balance Sheet: A Balance Sheet is a statement reflecting the assets and liabilities at a specific time.

Bookkeeping: The act of recording business transactions, including sales, income, expenses, payments, and more.

Bootstrapping: Starting a business with little or no startup funds is commonly referred to as bootstrapping the business.

Boutique: A Boutique operation is generally a small retail shop or service business operated with low square footage. They often target a niche customer and a higher than average price point.

Brand: A unique identifying symbol, name, or trademark, which allows consumers to distinguish one entity from another, is a Brand.

Brand Association: A thing, a place, a person, or even a feeling that consumers collectively associate with a specific brand is Brand Association.

Brand Loyalty: Brand Loyalty is having established customers who are reluctant to switch to competitor. This is generally associated with a great product, a great price point, or great customer service. It may also be associated with the Brand Association of a celebrity or role model.

Bread and Butter: The "Bread and Butter" of a company generally refers to its primarily source of revenue.

Breakeven Point: A Breakeven Point is a calculated point in which total income equals total cost. Therefore any income generated beyond the break-even point would produce a net profit.

Business Plan: A Business Plan is a document that summarizes the operational and financial objectives of a business and contains the detailed plans and budgets showing how the objectives are to be realized. It is a critical road map to ensuring all elements have been considered before starting operations, which increases the odds of success substantially.

Business To Business (B2B): Business conducted, including the sale or trade of goods, between one business and another, as opposed to between a business and an end user / consumer, or where one of the businesses is the end user / consumer.

Business To Consumer (B2C): Business conducted, including the sale or trade of goods, between a business and the end user / consumer, as opposed to between a business and another business which would act as a third party to the end user / consumer.

50

Calculated Risk: A risk taken after careful consideration, including variable probable outcomes or results.

Capital: The money invested into a business.

Capitalism: An economic system that is driven by individual businesses and corporations, rather than by the government.

Capital Asset: Any asset purchased as a long-term investment or for long-term use, like machinery or equipment, is considered a Capital Asset.

Cash Accounting: Cash Accounting is the simplest form of accounting, in which income is not recognized until it is received and expenses are not accounted for until they are paid.

Cash Cow: A dependable flow of income for a business that is generally used to fund the rest of the business.

Cash Flow: Cash Flow is the flow of money into and out of the business. It is important to maintain positive Cash Flow, which is when the inflow of money is higher than the outflow, on a regular basis.

Cash Flow Statement: A Cash Flow Statement is an accounting statement that presents how much, if any, of the cash generated by the business remains after expenses are paid.

Certified Public Accountant (CPA): A Certified Public Accountant is an accountant who has passed the uniformed CPA examination, administered by the American Institute of Certified Public Accountants, and who has received state certification to practice accounting. To do so, an accountant usually has to have five years of education at an accredited university and a specified amount of work experience. Furthermore, a CPA is typically required to complete a specified number of hours of continuing education each year to maintain the CPA certification.

Collateral: Anything of value that can be used to secure a loan or future obligation is Collateral.

Comparative Advantage: See Competitive Advantage

Competitive Advantage: A Competitive Advantage is an advantage over competitors gained by offering consumers greater value, either by means of lower prices or by providing greater benefits and service that justifies higher prices.

Competitive Analysis: A strategic marketing review of competitors, with specifics assessment of strengths, weaknesses, and each competitors place in the industry.

Conglomerate: A corporation that is made up of multiple smaller companies that generally vary in their business activities and industries.

Consultant: An expert individual or company that is hired by a business for analysis and guidance for reaching the company goals.

Consumer Price: The price the public will generally pay for a product or service.

Consumer Protection: Laws in place to protect consumers from unsafe and or defective products, deceitful marketing tactics, and dishonest companies as a whole.

Contract: A Contract is an agreement between two or more parties in which each agrees to perform certain actions and or compensate the other for their actions.

Contract Labor: Contract Labor is a person that is hired by a company, but not as an employee, to perform specific tasks for a specific period of time.

Contract Work: Contract Work is a person or company that is hired by a company, but not as en employee, to perform specific tasks for a specific period of time. It may also refer to the task the person or company was hired to do.

Controlling Interest: The ownership of more than 50% of a company, which allows for control in decision making and operational planning.

Cost Of Goods Sold (COGS): Total cost of products being sold in a retail or wholesale setting, or the total production cost, including labor, materials, and overhead, for manufactured goods or services.

COGS: See Cost Of Goods Sold

CPA: See Certified Public Accountant

Credit: Credit is term used to describe a delay in payment of goods or services based upon the sellers' confidence in the buyer's ability and intention to fulfill their financial obligations.

Creditor: The seller who delivers goods or services on credit, or the entity that provides funding to the seller on behalf of the buyer, is a Creditor.

EIN: See Employer Identification Number

Employer Identification Number (EIN): An Employer Identification Number or EIN is a number assigned to a business by the IRS for identification of all future federal tax related processes. It is obtained through the filing of federal form SS-4.

Entrepreneur: Although the definition is heavily debated, an Entrepreneur is anyone who starts or purchases and operates a business, assuming the financial responsibility and risks involved, and whose compensation is directly tied to the success of the business.

Equity: Equity is the amount vested to the owners or stockholders, generally described as the net difference between assets and liabilities.

Escrow: Most commonly known for its use in real estate purchases, Escrow is a temporary monetary deposit with a third party to be released to the other party as or when certain agreed upon conditions have been met.

Fiscal Year: A Fiscal Year is any twelve-month period that a company establishes as its accounting period. The twelve-month Calendar Year (January through December) is the most common twelve-month period designated, but should depend upon the accounting needs of the specific company.

Fixed Cost: Any cost that does not have a significant and direct relationship to production or sales volume is a Fixed Cost. The facility rent or mortgage is a great example. Generally speaking, a significant increase in production or sales would not cause your landlord to raise your rent or your bank to increase your mortgage payments.

For Profit: A For-Profit business is one that is the most common type of business entity, which includes S Corporations, LLC's, partnerships and other business forms. A For-Profit business is any business in which the owners or stockholders have or may have equity in the company. See Non Profit for the counter.

GAAP: See General Accepted Accounting Principles

General Partnerships: A General Partnership is a type of business entity in which two or more co-owners engage in business together, usually with a shared ownership of assets and a shared liability for company commitments and debts.

Generally Accepted Accounting Practices (GAAP): There are a common set of accounting principles, standards, and procedures that companies should commonly use to complete their financial statements, known as Generally Accepted Accounting Practices.

Gross Profit: Profits after cost of goods sold are deducted, but before any additional costs are factored in. This is calculated by subtracting the cost of goods sold from Gross Revenue. It is also known as Net Revenue.

Gross Revenue: Total money generated before any expenses are taken into account.

Internal Revenue Service (IRS): The IRS is the United States government agency responsible for the enforcement of tax laws and the collection of taxes.

IRS: See Internal Revenue Service

Joint Venture: A Joint Venture is a general partnership, typically formed to undertake a particular business transaction or project rather than one intended to continue indefinitely. Most often, these are used in real estate matters where two or more persons undertake to develop a specific piece of real property.

Keystone: When an item is sold at retail for twice the wholesale cost, it is said to be at Keystone pricing.

Labor Cost: The total of all wages paid to employees or sub-contractors, including salaries, employee benefits, and payroll taxes paid by the employer.

Leaseholder Improvements: Leasehold Improvements (sometimes referred to as "buildouts") are the structural changes you make to leased space to make it suitable for your business needs. For example, lighting changes, reception area, offices, dressing rooms, and other special rooms or partitions might be needed, as well as paint and carpeting/flooring. These costs may be paid by the landlord (and included in your monthly rent) or you may be able to make some changes yourself and save money.

Liabilities: Debt owed by the company, such as bank loans or accounts payable, are Liabilities.

Lien: A Lien is the legal right to hold property of another party or to have it sold or applied in payment of a claim. This is most commonly used in real estate transactions as leverage by the lending party.

Limited Liability Company (LLC): An LLC is a type of business entity that combines the corporate advantages of limited liability with the partnership advantage of pass-through taxation, where earnings are taxed only once.

Line of Credit: A revolving credit in which the funds can be re-used after repayment, usually with a low interest rate, is a Line of Credit.

LLC: See Limited Liability Company.

Marginal Cost: A Marginal Cost is the additional cost associated with producing one more unit of product.

Maturity: The date or time at which a loan becomes due is the loans date or time of Maturity.

Net Revenue: Profits after cost of goods sold are deducted, but before any additional costs are factored in. Calculated by subtracting cost of goods sold from Gross Revenue. Also known as Gross Profit.

Non-Profit: Unlike a for profit business, a Non-Profit is a corporation that cannot issue shares and cannot pay dividends. Categorized under the Federal Tax Code Section 501 (c) (3), a non-profit corporation is eligible for certain federal and state tax exemptions and, upon dissolution, must distribute its remaining assets to another non-profit group.

Open To Buy: Open To Buy is the amounted budgeted or planned to purchase additional goods for a specific period of time. This may be calculated by subtracting projected sales from current inventory levels and comparing that amount to the budgeted or planned inventory levels for the same time frame. The difference between projected inventory levels and planned inventory levels is the amount in which you are Open To Buy.

Overhead: Overhead is business expenses not directly related to a particular good or service produced. A common example is utilities.

Owner/ Operator: A business that has an Owner/ Operator has an owner who also is the primary employee or staff member managing the daily operations. Therefore, the owner is an owner/operator.

P & L Statement: See Profit & Loss Statement.

POP: See Point Of Purchase.

Point Of Purchase (POP): The Point of Purchase is the location in which the customer or end user makes the buying decision. On a macro scale this is the retailer or geographical area in which the decision is made. More commonly referred to on the micro level, this is the specific area in which the decision is made. A particular display, feature, or cash register areas could all POP's.

Preferred Lenders: Banks or lending institutions that are approved by the SBA to make a guaranteed SBA loan without prior SBA approval are known as Preferred Lenders.

Private Label Brand: A Private Label Brand is a product owned and marketed specifically for a particular retailer or supplier. The manufacturer is contracted to produce the product and, many times, physically label it with the purchaser's brand. The manufacturer, however, does not own the rights to the brand.

Pro Forma: Pro Forma is the Latin term meaning For The Sake of Form. In the financial world it is used to describe an accounting calculation displayed on a financial statement for a current statistic or future projection.

Profit & Loss (P & L) Statement: A financial document that lists income, expenses, and the net profit or loss is the Profit & Loss Statement, or P & L, or income statement.

Return on Investment (ROI): Return on Investment, or ROI, is the profit generated by the money a business owner puts into the business. ROI is usually expressed as a percentage return. It can be calculated by dividing the company's annual income or profit by the amount of the original investment (or current investment). ROI may also be expressed in terms of "opportunity cost," or the return that the owner gave up to invest in the company. ROI may also be expressed in terms of a specific amount of money for a specific project

Revenue Stream: A Revenue Stream is a specific source or specific product that is used to generate revenue. Many businesses will have several revenue streams like a product for sale and a service provided.

ROI: See Return on Investment.

S Corporation: Like a C Corporation, an S Corporation is its own legal entity, protecting its shareholders from legal liability and avoiding double taxation.

SBA: See Small Business Administration.

SCORE: See Service Corps of Retired Executives.

Security Deposit: A Security Deposit is money set aside or paid in advance to secure the lenders interest. This is most common with rent, utilities, phone, and cable. The landlord or utility provider will require two months security deposit to start. This money is then used for the final month of your service or returned to you at the appropriate time.

Service Corps of Retired Executives (SCORE): SCORE is a 10,500-member volunteer association sponsored by the Small Business Administration (SBA), which matches volunteer business-management counselors with present prospective small business owners in need of expert advice.

SIC: See Standard Industrial Classification Code.

SKU: See Stock Keeping Unit.

Small Business Administration (SBA): The Small Business Administration, or SBA, is a federal agency that seeks to aid, council, assist, and protects the interests of small business. SBA participates in a number of loan programs designed for the final month of your service or returned to you at the appropriate time.

Sole Proprietor: A Sole Proprietor business is not a separate entity from the owner. A sole proprietor directly owns the business and is 100% in control. The owner is also directly responsible for its debts and any tax liability.

Standard Industrial Classification Code (SIC): An SIC number is a four-digit number assigned to identify a business based on the type of business or trade involved. The first two digits correspond to major groups such as construction and manufacturing, while the last two digits correspond to subgroup of the industry. SIC numbers are published by the U.S. Department of Commerce.

Staple Product: A Staple Product is any product that is core to a business. These items are basic necessities to customers, in that field, and usually attribute a majority of a retailer's volume.

Stock Keeping Unit (SKU): A Stock Keeping Unit is a string of characters, most often numbers and or letters that identify an individual item. This is generally specific to a particular size, color, shape, model, etc. A manufacturer or retailers SKU count is the number of different items sold.

Target Market: A Target Market is a specific group of potential customers which you have identified who have needs or problems which your products or services can fulfill.

Tax Number: A Tax Number is assigned to a business by the state in which it is established, to enable the business to buy wholesale and avoid paying sales tax on goods and products.

Term Loan: A loan written for a specific term, like 60 months, calling for a monthly principal and interest payments is a Term Loan.

Time Loan: A loan written for a set time period, like 60 months, calling for all principal and interest due at maturity is a Time Loan.

Trade Fixture: A Trade Fixture is a piece of equipment on or attached to the real estate which is used in a trade or business.

Triple Net: Triple Net is a rental term or type in which the tenant pays rent to the landlord and additionally assumes responsibility for all costs regarding the operation, taxes and maintenance of the premises and building.

Turn: Turn or Inventory Turn is the number of times inventory is sold and replaced in a set time frame. This could be calculated and utilized for all inventory, by brand, by product group, and even down to the individual SKU.

Variable Cost: Any cost that has a significant and direct relationship to production or sales volume is a Variable Cost.

Vendor: A supplier or seller of a specific product line. Vendor is usually interchangeable with the word supplier.

Venture Capital: Money used to support a new venture, either supporting equity, risk or as investment capital.

CHAPTER 16:
MORE SUPPORTING DOCUMENTS

Section 15: Supporting Documents might also include information specific to funding plans. This does not include spreadsheets of expenses and start-up costs. Those should only be in Section 12: Cash Flow / Projections. The information contained in Section 15 should be limited to supporting information, like the SBA Info Sheet below and applications for funding.

Modify the paragraphs below for your business.

SMALL BUSINESS ADMINISTRATION

(SBA)

The Small Business Administration does far more for entrepreneurs than most people know. In additional to the SBA Loans that most people know of, the SBA is a wonderful source for information, guidance, and contacts, before startup and as you grow. Furthermore, the SBA Loans themselves are commonly misunderstood, but extremely valuable.

The SBA itself does not lend money to businesses. Instead, they work closely with banks and lending institutions, known as partners, to minimize their risk in lending you, the entrepreneur, the funds needed to start or grow your business. By implementing specific standards and requirements, SBA assists their partners in finding sound investments in their community, which gives you the opportunity to make your dreams come true.

According to www.sba.gov, the 7(a) Loan may be used to establish a new business or to assist in the acquisition, operation, or expansion of an existing business. Specifically it could be used for: the purchase of land or buildings, to cover new construction as well as expansion or conversion of existing facilities, the purchase of equipment, machinery, furniture, fixtures, supplies, or materials, as long-term working capital, including the payment of accounts payable and/or the purchase of inventory, as short-term working capital needs, including seasonal financing, contract performance, construction financing and export production, or to purchase an existing business

The SBA is located in Washington, DC and can be reached by phone at 1-800-827-5722. The SBA is broken in 10 Region offices and dozens of local offices. The following map outlines the states grouped for each region. For more information, or to find an office near you, visit www.sba.gov.

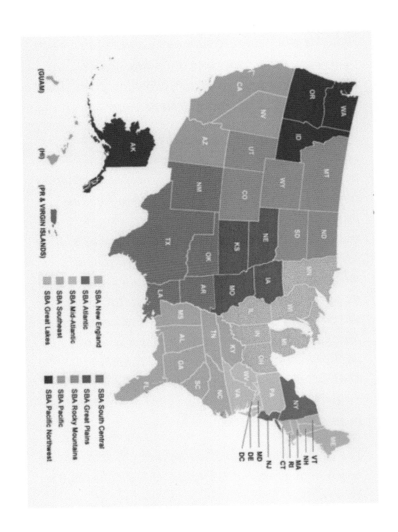

(GUAM)

(HI)

(PR & VIRGIN ISLANDS)

SBA New England
SBA Atlantic
SBA Mid-Atlantic
SBA Southeast
SBA Great Lakes

SBA South Central
SBA Great Plains
SBA Rocky Mountains
SBA Pacific
SBA Pacific Northwest

68

CHAPTER 17:
PUTTING TOGETHER YOUR FINAL PLAN

By now you are familiar with each of the fifteen sections that make a complete business plan. You have also seen that the majority of it has been completed for you. By transcribing much of this book into your own plan you will be ready to seek funding or start your business.

But before you do, here are a few additional notes to help put it all together.

When compiling your final business plan we recommend that you use a standard 1/2" (.125 cm) three ring binder, with a clear sleeve on the cover. Make your cover sheet very simple with large block letters that say the name of your business and identify it as a business plan. Put it in the clear cover on the front of your binder. The picture below shows the cover sheet for Springfield Interior Design. Be sure to include your basic contact information, like address, phone number, email address, and web address. Also include a statement of privacy to ensure that the reader understands the importance of confidentiality. The Springfield Interior Design business plan put the following disclaimer.

The information provided by SPRINGFIELD INTERIOR DESIGN in this business plan is unique to this business and confidential; therefore, anyone reading this plan agrees not to disclose any of the information in this business plan, proprietary or otherwise, without the written permission of SPRINGFIELD INTERIOR DESIGN.

SPRINGFIELD

INTERIOR DESIGN

BUSINESS PLAN

SPRINGFIELD INTERIOR DESIGN

SPRINGFIELD, MO.

WWW.SPRINGFIELDDESIGN.COM

INFO@SPRINGFIELDDESIGN.COM

The Table of Contents should go in the binder as the very first inside page, to help make navigation through your business plan easier. The picture below shows the Table of Contents for the Springfield Interior Design business plan.

TABLE OF CONTENTS

The remaining pages should be placed in their respective section of the business plan. We recommend using 15 section divider tabs to make navigation through your business plan easier for you and your banker or investor.

Once again, congratulations on taking one of the biggest steps of your life. You are well on your way down the path to building wealth and making all your dreams come true.

If you have any questions or want to share your story -- feel free to contact us via email or through any of our social media channels.

Facebook: Facebook/InDemandBusinessPlans

Instagram: @In_Demand_Business_Plans

Twitter: @Twitter In_Demand_BP

Email: InDemandMarketing @ Yahoo.com

The In Demand Business Plans Facebook page and Instagram page has a ton of motivational content, as well as information and support for small, start-up businesses. DM us and let us know how your business progresses. We would be glad to help promote.

You truly have taken a big step forward to changing your life. Now, rather than work on a business plan for months, you can get started quickly on achieving your goals and building wealth. We wish you luck, even though a solid, in depth, but simple business plan takes much of the need for luck out of the equation. We would love to hear about your success in the future.

Although it has been attributed to many including Benjamin Franklin, Winston Churchill's version is perhaps the most relevant here. "He who fails to plan is planning to fail." By reading this book you have jumped miles ahead in the planning process and are now poised for success.

Other Business Plans Available From
In Demand Business Plans
Include:

Bike Shop

Flower Shop / Florist

Used Bookstore

$1 (One Dollar) Bookstore

Upscale Men's Resale Shop

Bicycle Repair Shop

Computer Repair Shop

Upscale Women's Resale Shop

Lawnmower & Small Engine Repair Shop

New Baby Store

Camera & Photography Shop

Pet Store

Furniture Repair Center

Upscale Children's Resale Shop

Vacuum Cleaner Repair Center

Pool Supply Store

Camera Repair Center

New & Used Video Game Store

Gym

Skate Shop

Payroll & Bookkeeping Service

Portrait Studio

Jeans Resale Shop

Baby Boutique

$1 (One Dollar) Jewelry Store

Beauty Supply Store

New Baby Store

Camera & Photography Shop

Pet Store

Bridal Shop

Tanning Salon

Hair Salon

Used Entertainment Store

Dance Studio

Massage Business

Tile Installation

Mobile Computer Repair Business

Patio Installation

Housekeeping Service

Painting Service

Automotive Repair Center

Thrift Store

Used Musical Instrument Store

Pizza Business

Ice Cream Shop

Party Supply Store

Carpet Installation

Donut Shop

Sandwich Shop

Picture Frame Store

Auto Body Repair Center

Drywall & Insulation Installation

Nail Salon

Christian Bookstore

Hobby & Toy Store

Home Furnishings Store

Mowing & Lawn Care Business

Landscaping Company

Hardware Store

Sunglasses Shop

Perfume Shop

Maternity Wear Shop

Lingerie Shop

Supplement Store

Lighting Store

Fence Construction

Roofing & Roof Repair

Complete Carpet Cleaning

Pest Control

Martial Arts Studio